WHITNEY

The History and Activities of the

WAGON TRAIL

Lisa Klobuchar

Heinemann Library
Chicago, Illinois

Customer Service 888-454-2279
Visit our website at www.heinemannlibrary.com

Designed by Richard Parker and Tinstar Design Ltd (www.tinstar.co.uk)
Printed and bound in China by WKT Company Limited

10 09 08 07 06
10 9 8 7 6 5 4 3 2 1

Library of Congress Cataloging-in-Publication Data

Klobuchar, Lisa.
  The history and activities of the wagon trail / Lisa Klobuchar.
      p. cm. -- (Hands-on American history)
  Includes bibliographical references and index.
  ISBN 1-4034-6055-8 -- ISBN 1-4034-6062-0 (pbk.)
  1. Frontier and pioneer life--West (U.S.)--Study and teaching--Activity programs--Juvenile literature. 2. West (U.S.)--History--19th century--Study and teaching--Activity programs--Juvenile literature. 3. West (U.S.)--Social life and customs--19th century--Study and teaching--Activity programs--Juvenile literature. I. Title. II. Series.
  F596.K59 2005
  978--dc22
                              2004003879

Acknowledgments
The author and publishers are grateful to the following for permission to reproduce copyright material: Bridgeman Art Library p. 9 (Private Collection); Corbis pp. 12, 17 (Bettmann), 24 (David Muench), 14 (Lowell Georgia), 18, 28; Getty Images pp. 8 (Time Life Pictures), 10, 11; Harcourt Education pp. 19, 23, 27 (Janet Moran); Imageworks p. 16; National Cowboy Museum p. 20 (Devere Hlefrich Rodeo Photocollection); North Wind Picture Archives pp. 4, 5, 7, 13, 15.

Cover photographs by Corbis/David Muench and Library of Congress

Every effort has been made to contact copyright holders of any material reproduced in this book. Any omissions will be rectified in subsequent printings if notice is given to the publishers.

Contents

Chapter 1: Bound for New Lands 4

Chapter 2: Days and Nights on the Trail 10

Chapter 3: Travelers at Play..........................16

Chapter 4: Hands-on History 18

Recipe: Make Spotted Pup..........................18

Craft: Make Braided Tack 20

Craft: Make a Prairie Schooner 24

Craft: Make a Buzz Saw 28

Glossary..........................30

More Books to Read..........................30

A Note to Teachers..........................31

Index 32

Some words are shown in bold, **like this**. You can find out
what they mean by looking in the glossary.

Chapter 1: Bound for New Lands

The 1800s were a time of major growth for the United States. In 1800, the United States stretched westward only as far as the Mississippi River. But then, between 1803 and 1853, the size of the country tripled through land purchase and warfare.

Growth of a nation

In the early 1800s, everything west of the Mississippi River was open **frontier**. To easterners it was a mysterious, unknown wilderness. In 1803 President Thomas Jefferson bought a vast area of land from the French. The land deal was called the Louisiana Purchase. It extended the United States to include all the territory from Canada to the Gulf of Mexico and from the Mississippi Valley to the Rocky Mountains.

This map shows Lewis and Clark's trail.

TIME LINE

1803	1804–1806	1840	1842	1845
President Thomas Jefferson makes the Louisiana Purchase.	Lewis and Clark explore the Louisiana Territory.	First group of settlers start the journey westward in covered wagons.	Oregon trail opens.	Texas becomes part of the United States. More than 3,000 settlers have traveled west on the Oregon trail.

The next year, President Jefferson sent a team of explorers led by army captains Meriwether Lewis and William Clark to explore the region. Jefferson directed Lewis and Clark to form relationships with the Native American groups living there, to draw maps, and to make scientific observations on the land, weather, plants, and animals.

The expedition set off in May 1804 from St. Louis, Missouri. The team canoed up the Missouri River, crossed the Rockies, and reached the Pacific coast of Oregon in November 1805. They started their homeward journey the following spring and arrived in St. Louis in September 1806. Their trip totaled 8,000 miles (12,875 kilometers).

1846	1848	1861–1865	1869	1870s
United States gets the southern part of Oregon territory from Great Britain.	Gold is discovered in California, drawing many people west.	Civil War is fought.	Transcontinental railroad is completed.	Oregon trail is abandoned.

Lewis and Clark's expedition was important in many ways. The team gathered valuable knowledge. The trip also opened up the territory beyond the Louisiana Purchase and allowed the United States to claim it as well. This set the stage for the great age of westward settlement that went on from the mid- to late 1800s. In 1853 the size of the country doubled again, as the United States took over lands west of the Rocky Mountains, all the way to the Pacific Ocean. With that addition, the country's borders looked much as they do today.

Blazing westward trails

Beginning about 1840, large numbers of Americans and settlers from other countries began pouring into the lands west of the Mississippi River. They traveled more than 2,000 miles (3,219 kilometers) along the Oregon, California, and Mormon trails. They settled the far western areas first. It was only after 1860 that settlers started staking claims in the vast Great Plains region in the middle of the country.

This map shows some of the more common wagon trails.

KEY
— Oregon Trail
— Mormon Trail
— California Trails
— Boundaries as of 1860

The settlers left their homes for many reasons. Many had heard reports of attractive land regions, fertile farmlands, and mild climates and wanted to start farms. Others went simply to make a fresh start in a new, untamed land. After gold was discovered in California in 1848, many others came with the hope of finding enough gold to become instantly rich. In all, more than 500,000 settlers, including 250,000 children, made the difficult and exhausting trip in wagon trains over wilderness trails.

A page from William Clark's travel journal.

The first of these settlers were a group of 50 people, including 10 children, who bravely set off from Independence, Missouri, in 1841. These settlers were bound for new lives in Oregon and California. At that time, there was no trail for them to follow. They simply followed the course of the Platte River from Nebraska to Colorado. They kept their wagons pointed west toward the setting sun. In southeastern Idaho, the group split in two. One group went southwest and ended up in California. The second continued northwest to Oregon.

The northwest branch of the trail the settlers blazed became known as the Oregon Trail, and its southwestern branch became the California Trail. Most wagon-train travelers followed these routes. The settlers began their journeys at a few towns along the Mississippi River. These starting points, called jumping-off places, included Nauvoo, Illinois; Council Bluffs, Iowa; St. Joseph, Missouri; and Liberty, Missouri. The most important among these was Independence, Missouri.

Setting out

The westward journey took about six months, and travelers had to leave at just the right time. If they left too early in the spring, there would not be enough grass for their animals to eat along the way. If they left too late, they risked being caught in the mountains when the snows started. As a result, the wagon trains usually left the jumping-off places sometime in May, with the hope of arriving in California or Oregon by November.

This pioneer wagon is filled with clothes, furniture, and other posessions.

A 19th century wagon train.

The most important piece of equipment for any settlers heading west was a sturdy, well-equipped wagon. The wagon measured about 10 to 12 feet (3 to 4 meters) long and 6 feet (2 meters) wide, with sides 2 to 3 feet (61 to 91 centimeters) high. The body of the wagon was designed to float so that it could be used as a boat when rivers had to be crossed. At the start of the journey, the wagons would be loaded with 2,500 pounds (1,134 kilograms) of supplies.

Teams of strong, healthy oxen usually pulled the heavy wagons. Horses and mules were not used. Horses were not strong enough, and mules were hard to control. Neither horses nor mules could survive well on the tough prairie grasses that grew along the trail. But oxen, bulls that were specially bred to be big, strong, and gentle, were perfect for the job. They were strong enough to pull the wagons, easy to control, and could munch happily on prairie grass.

Still, some horses did come along on the trip. Scouts rode horses ahead of the wagon train to find good places to camp for the night. Sometimes men and boys rode horses to hunt buffalo when they spotted a herd.

9

Chapter 2: Days and Nights on the Trail

The trail west was not a lonely, empty road. In fact, the route was sometimes so crowded that travelers had a hard time finding good camping places. The dust kicked up by so many wagons and the hooves of so many animals made it hard to breathe. In some ways it was like a traveling party, with cooperation, play, disagreements, danger, and discovery. Most wagon trains chose a leader to make important decisions for the group.

Stopping and going

The days on the trail started early, usually around 4 A.M. Everyone pitched in to build fires, prepare breakfast, hitch up the animals, and collect water. After a filling breakfast of beans, cornbread, bacon, and hot coffee, the wagon train was under way by 7 A.M.

The wagons moved along at a very slow pace. Men usually walked with the oxen. Most settlers walked alongside the wagons. Only very young children, new mothers, old people, and the sick or injured rode in the wagons. There were two

A wagon train makes its way west. A woman walks alongside the oxen, urging them on with a whip.

A wagon train forms a defensive circle at Camp Comanche, a traders' camp on the Santa Fe Trail, between the North Fork and the Canadian River. A line of soldiers guards the camp from attack.

main reasons for this. First, the wagons were usually packed tightly with the supplies needed for the long journey. Second, the travelers wanted to spare the oxen from any unnecessary weight. So most of the people made the 2,000-mile (3,219-kilometer) trip almost entirely on foot.

As time for the midday rest stop neared, riders on horseback would ride ahead. Their job was to pick out a good spot for the settlers to have lunch and rest the animals. After a while, they set off again. Late in the afternoon, it was time to set up camp for the night. Usually the leader of the wagon train would direct the wagons where to park. He would form the wagons into a big circle. This made it easier to keep everyone in the group together. If there were enough wagons, the circle was big enough to form a **corral** to keep the animals inside.

At the campsite, the men would make necessary repairs to the wagons, while the women cooked. Children helped out by collecting firewood, milking the cows, caring for younger children, mending and washing clothing, and tending to the livestock.

Dining on the trail

For settlers traveling in wagon trains along the westward trails, cooking in the open was a way of life. As a result, meals were simple, and every meal was very much like the last.

Another reason the meals were so plain on the wagon train was because the settlers only brought foods that would not spoil on the long trip. Families packed cornmeal, rice, flour, salted pork, dried fruit, beans, and coffee into their wagons. They had to do without fresh foods such as fruits, vegetables, and eggs.

This family cooks by campfire while a wagon train passes in the background.

On the wagon train, the women did the cooking. In the morning, a woman might make some kind of bread or cake made of cornmeal, such as cornbread, johnnycakes, or pancakes. With these she would serve bacon, gravy made by adding flour and milk to bacon grease, and hot, strong coffee. She often slow-cooked beans overnight in the embers of the evening fire, as well. Settlers enjoyed meat when the men and boys shot jackrabbit, buffalo, pronghorn, prairie chicken, or other prairie animals. They also ate berries and nuts collected by the children along the trail. Cooks sometimes served rice with dinner and desserts sweetened with dried fruits.

Settlers lucky enough to have a milking cow with them could make butter by attaching a jug of cream to the back of their wagon. A day of jostling over the bumpy trails turned the cream to butter.

A family heads west with its belongings and animals.

Dangers and hardships

Only nine out of every ten travelers who set off in wagon trains made it to their destinations. They faced many hardships, but most were not life threatening. Travelers suffered from sunburn and insect bites and were always choking on dust. Storms sometimes dropped large hailstones and sent down bolts of lightning. Sometimes, because of bad planning or bad luck, travelers found themselves without enough food and suffered from poor nutrition.

Those few who did not survive the trip were the victims of accidents and illness. Travelers were injured or even killed after being run over by a heavy wagon. People sometimes accidentally shot themselves when they did not handle guns and rifles safely. Crossing rivers was especially dangerous, and settlers and animals sometimes drowned.

This pioneer grave still exists along the original Oregon trail. The original gravemaker, a wagon wheel, has been replaced.

This is an artist's idea of a peaceful meeting between pioneers and Native Americans.

By far the greatest danger to pioneers on the westward trails was illness. Though the settlers did not know it back then, germs called **bacteria** cause many diseases. Spoiled food and dirty water contain a lot of bacteria. Settlers drank from streams polluted with animal and human waste. They camped among the garbage and waste left by earlier travelers. They sometimes had to eat spoiled food. As a result, outbreaks of a disease called **cholera** sometimes occurred. Cholera could kill a person in less than one day.

Some people believe that Native Americans were a great danger to the pioneers. But this is not really true. Most of the time the settlers and Native Americans left each other alone. Though there were a few violent clashes between settlers and Native Americans, more Native Americans were killed by settlers than the other way around.

Chapter 3: Travelers at Play

The journey west with a wagon train was hard work and sometimes even dangerous. But children and adults also made time for fun. For many children, the trip was the adventure of a lifetime.

Children on the trail often ran back and forth from wagon to wagon, playing, visiting old friends and making new ones. There was always something new to explore. Sometimes they would stop along the way to look at an unusual plant or animal. **Souvenir** hunting often went along with these side trips. Children might collect feathers or colorful rocks, pretty wildflowers, or a small animal bone. These interesting objects formed collections that helped pioneer children remember their amazing journey. Children also sometimes kept small animals they found and cared for them as pets.

Life on the wagon trail could be fun for children.

Pioneers resting on the Oregon trail.

Other kids amused themselves in more exciting ways. They would ride under the wagons on spare tent poles or wheel **axles**. Or they would ride on the wagon tongue, which was the piece of wood that stuck out from the front of the wagon. They would stand on the tongue and put their hands on the back of an ox for balance.

Kids played checkers, jacks, cards, marbles, ball games, hoop-and-stick, tag, and hide-and-seek. Pioneer kids' toys were small and almost always homemade. Children's toys included rag dolls, cornhusk dolls, and bow-and-arrow sets.

During the brief time between the end of evening chores and bedtime was the only chance adults had to play. Playing instruments, singing, and dancing provided fun and relaxation at the end of a hard day on the trail. Brigham Young, who led many Mormon settlers from the Midwest to Utah, encouraged settlers to play music and dance as a way to lift their spirits. The families and individuals who traveled west helped build the country we have today. Life for them could be hard, but it could also be fun.

Chapter 4: Hands-on History

By doing the hands-on activities and crafts in this chapter, you'll get a feel for what life was like for people who lived, worked, and traveled on the wagon trail.

Recipe: Make Spotted Pup

If a family was able to bring a cow along on the trail, they could have fresh milk. Rice and dried fruit were easy to bring along. All these ingredients go into a delicious rice pudding with raisins that pioneers called spotted pup.

This group of cowboys is enjoying a meal along the banks of the Yellowstone River in Montana.

1. Put the rice, milk, brown sugar, and salt into the saucepan and stir.

2. Put the burner on medium heat and bring the mixture to a boil.

3. Turn the burner down to low heat and cover the pan. Cook for 20 minutes.

4. Stir in the raisins and cook for 10 minutes longer.

5. Serve in small bowls with cinnamon sprinkled on top.

INGREDIENTS AND SUPPLIES

- 4-quart nonstick saucepan with lid
- wooden or plastic spoon
- 3/4 cup uncooked rice
- 4 cups milk
- 3/4 cup brown sugar
- 1/4 teaspoon salt
- 1 cup raisins
- cinnamon

Craft: Make Braided Tack

Travelers on a wagon train needed to fasten gear to their wagons and to their horses. Rope worked well to fasten gear to the wagons. But to fasten gear to a horse or to fasten teams of oxen to a wagon, it was best to use **tack**, or leather straps. Cowboys were especially skilled at braiding tack from strips of **rawhide**, or leather.

WARNING!

Make sure to read all the directions before starting the project.

This modern cowboy is making braided tack.

SUPPLIES

- leather or suede cord (or shoelaces)
- round key ring about 1 inch (2.5 cm) in diameter
- clothes hanger
- large bead or small wooden spool
- white glue (or hot glue with adult help)

A

B

1. Cut two pieces of leather cord 6 feet (183 centimeters) long.

2. Fold one of the lengths of leather in half. Pass the folded end through the key ring from front to back and then pass the loose ends forward through the leather loop that is created. (See Picture A)

3. Repeat this step with the other length of leather. Now you should have four strands 3 feet (91 centimeters) long. All the strands should be hanging from the key ring. (See Picture B)

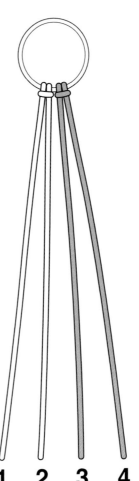

1   2   3   4

4. Hook the key ring around a
   hanger and hook the hanger
   onto a doorknob or some other
   object so that it will be held
   firmly as you braid.

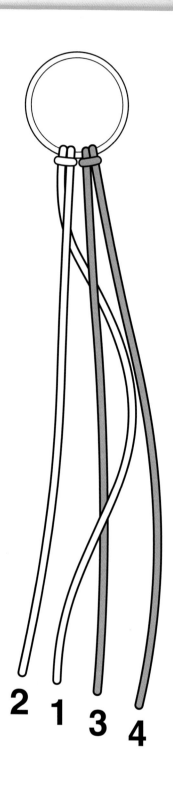

5. Move the strand at the far left
   behind the other strands. Bring
   it forward between the strands
   in the third and fourth position,
   and pass it over the second
   strand. (See Picture C)

6. Move the strand at the far
   right between the other
   strands. Bring it forward
   between the strands in the
   first and second positions, and
   pass it over the second strand.
   *Why does braiding make the
   tack stronger?*

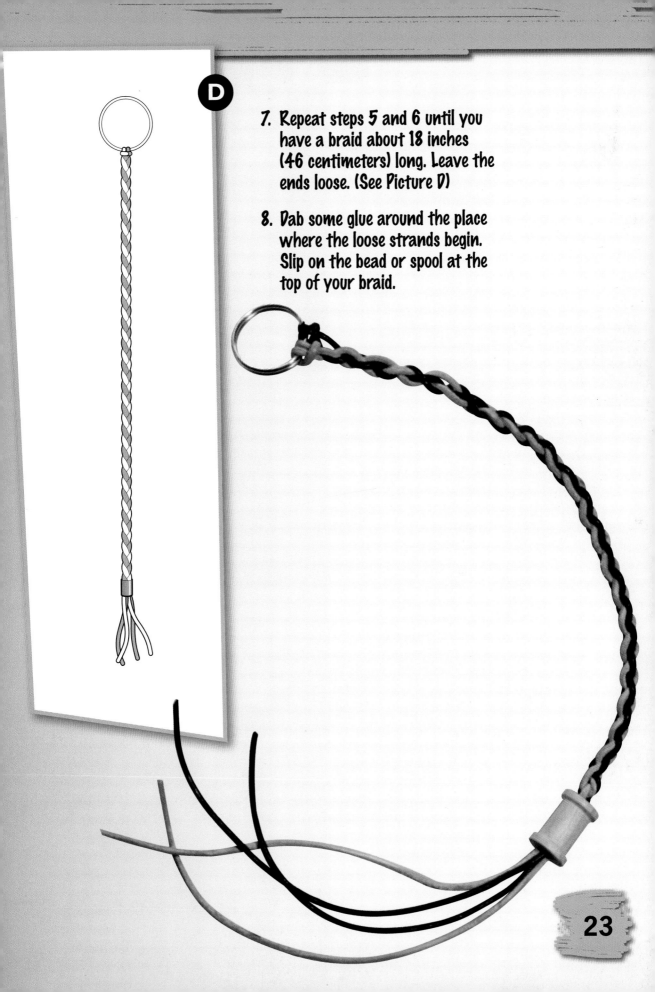

D

7. Repeat steps 5 and 6 until you have a braid about 18 inches (46 centimeters) long. Leave the ends loose. (See Picture D)

8. Dab some glue around the place where the loose strands begin. Slip on the bead or spool at the top of your braid.

Craft: Make a Prairie Schooner

To some people, Conestoga wagons, with their waterproof white canvas coverings, looked like ships at sea as they crossed the prairie. For this reason, they became known as prairie **schooners**.

WARNING!

Make sure to read all the directions before starting the project.

1. Cut two pieces of dowel about 1.5 inches (4 centimeters) longer than the width of the shoebox lid. Glue them to the top of the lid about 1 inch (2.5 centimeters) from each end, as shown. Turn the shoebox lid over so the dowels are on the table. This will be the body of your wagon. (See Picture A)

2. Cut four strips from the posterboard or thin cardboard, each about 1 inch (2.5 centimeters) wide and about 14 inches (36 centimeters) long. Bend these into U-shapes.

SUPPLIES

- posterboard (or thin cardboard from a cereal box)
- shoebox lid (or similarly shaped cardboard)
- scissors (or craft knife with adult help)
- stapler
- strong white glue (or hot glue with adult help)
- clear tape
- cardboard (from a shoebox or other source)
- brown paint
- white cloth, about 15 inches by 15 inches (38 centimeters by 38 centimeters)
- 2 pieces of string or yarn, about 16 inches (41 centimeters) long
- 1/4-inch (6-milimeter) wooden dowel, or rod
- brown construction paper (optional)
- hole punch (optional)

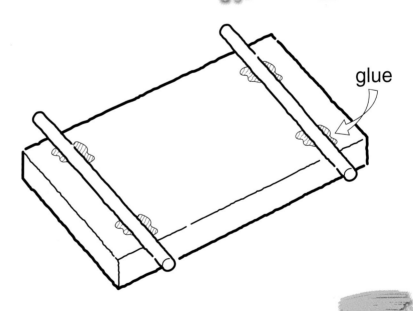

glue

A

3. Glue and tape the cardboard strips to the inside of the wagon body. Set the wagon aside to let the glue dry completely.

4. Cut four wheels from cardboard. Make two wheels slightly larger than the other two.

5. Paint the wagon and the wheels brown, or glue on brown construction paper. *How can you make the wagon look like it is made from slats of wood?*

6. Use a hole punch, scissors, or ask an adult to help poke holes in the center of the wheels. The holes should be small enough so that the dowels will fit in snugly.

7. Cut four dime-sized circles from the construction paper or from the thin cardboard. These will be the caps that hold the wheels onto the dowels.

8. Insert one end of a dowel into the hole in the center of a wheel, so it is even with the outside of the wheel. Glue one of the construction paper circles over the end of the dowel. Repeat this step with the other three wheels. Put the larger wheels on the back of the wagon and the smaller wheels on the front. (See Picture B)

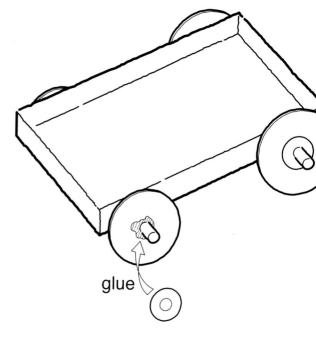

glue

9. Cut the piece of cloth to fit over the top of the wagon. Place a piece of string on the cloth, near the edge. Fold the cloth over the string to create a hem, or tunnel, for the string inside. Glue or staple the cloth down so it stays in place. Do the same thing at the other end of the cloth.

10. Glue the cloth over the top of the wagon. When the glue is dry, pull the string snug to create a gathered opening on each side. (See Picture C)

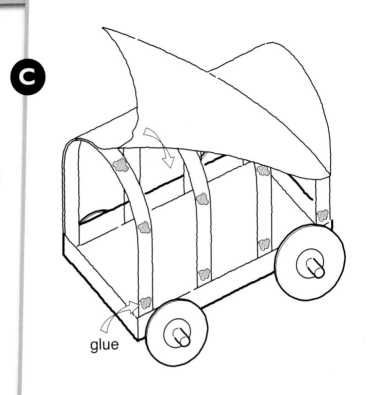

C

glue

Craft: Make a Buzz Saw

Toys that children played with on the wagon train had to be small and easy to carry. They were almost always handmade. Buzz saws, known in some places as whirligigs, were easy to carry and could be played with while walking. Most buzz saws were made with wood, but you will use a button.

SUPPLIES

- piece of string about twice as long as your arm
- large button (at least 3 inches) with two holes in the middle

Most toys on the wagon trail were made from wood or other simple materials.

1. Thread the string through the button holes and tie the ends in a knot, forming a loop. (See Picture A)

2. Hold each end of the string so that the button hangs loosely in the middle.

3. Swing the button in a circle to tightly wind up the string. (See Picture B)

4. Pull your hands apart and push them together again. The button will twirl and make noise. *What causes the button to make noise?*

This toy can also be made using a small, flat piece of wood with two holes drilled in it, instead of a button. If you use wood, you may wish to decorate it with markers or stickers.

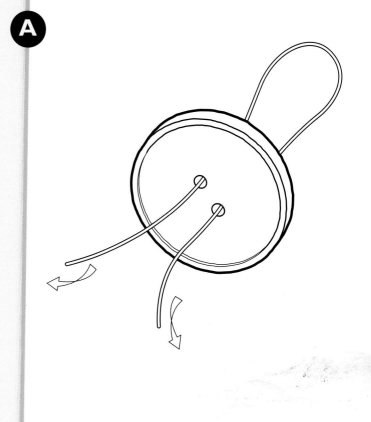

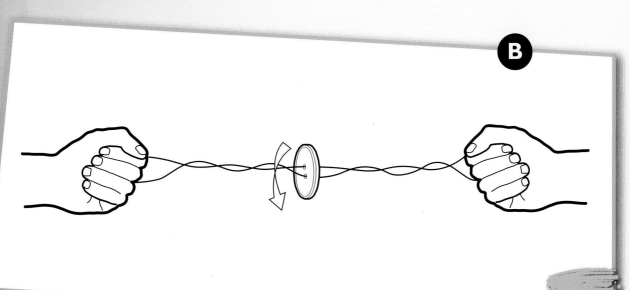

Glossary

axle long rod that attaches wheels on a wagon

bacteria a type of living thing that is too small to be seen without a microscope

cholera deadly disease caused by drinking unclean water or eating unclean food

corral fenced-in area in which horses or livestock are kept

frontier unsettled land

rawhide animal skin that has had all hair removed but has not been tanned into leather

schooner oceangoing ship with two sails

souvenir small object that a person collects on a trip to keep as a way to remember the trip

tack leather straps and other things used to fasten gear to a saddle

More Books to Read

Herbert, Janice. *Lewis and Clark for Kids: Their Journey of Discovery with 21 Activities.* Chicago: Chicago Review Press, 2003.

Isaacs, Sally Senzell. *The Oregon Trail.* Chicago: Heinemann Library, 2003.

Morley, Jacqueline. *You Wouldn't Want to Be an American Pioneer!* New York: Franklin Watts, 2002.

A Note to Teachers

The instructions for these projects are designed to allow students to work as independently as possible. However, it is always a good idea to make a prototype before assigning any project, so that students can see how their own work will look when completed. Prior to introducing these projects, teachers should collect and prepare the materials and be ready for any modifications that may be necessary. Participating in the project-making process will help teachers understand the directions and be ready to assist students with difficult steps. Teachers might also choose to adapt or modify the lessons to better suit the needs of an individual student or class. No one knows what levels of achievement students will reach better than their teacher.

While it is preferable for students to work as independently as possible, there is some flexibility in regards to project materials and tools. They can vary according to what is available. For instance, while standard white glue may be most familiar to students, there might be times when a teacher will choose to speed up a project by using a hot glue gun to fasten materials for students. Likewise, while a project may call for leather cord, it is feasible in most instances to substitute vinyl cord or even yarn or rope. Acrylic paint may be recommended because it adheres better to a material like felt or plastic, but other types of paint would be useable as well. Circles can be drawn with a compass, or simply by tracing a cup, roll of tape, or other circular object. Obviously, allowing students a broad spectrum of creativity and opportunities to problem-solve within the parameters of a given project will encourage their critical thinking skills most fully.

Each project contains an italicized question somewhere in the directions. These questions are meant to be thought-provoking and promote discussion while students work on the project.

Index

accidents 14

buffalo 9
buzz saw 28–29

California Trail 6, 8
camping places 9, 10, 11
children 11, 16–17
cholera 15

daily life 10–13
dangers and hardships 10, 14–15
defensive circles 11

food and cooking 10, 12–13, 14,
    15, 18–19

gold 5, 7
Great Plains 6

horses and mules 9, 20
hunting 9, 13

illness 15
Independence, Missouri 8

Jefferson, Thomas 4, 5
jumping-off places 8

leisure time 16–17
Lewis and Clark expedition 4, 5, 6, 7
Louisiana Purchase 4, 6

Mississippi River 4, 6
Mormon Trail 6, 17
music and dance 17

Native Americans 5, 15

Oregon Trail 4, 5, 6, 8, 14
oxen 9, 10, 11

prairie schooners 24–27

spotted pup 18–19
supplies 9, 11, 12

tack, braided 20–23
timeline 4–5
toys and games 16, 17, 28–29

wagon trails (map) 6
wagon train leaders 10, 11
wagon trains 7, 8–17
wagons 8, 9, 11, 24–27

Young, Brigham 17